CAMPAIGN FINANCING AND POLITICAL FREEDOM

Ralph K. Winter, Jr.
in association with John R. Bolton

American Enterprise Institute for Public Policy Research
Washington, D. C.

Ralph K. Winter, Jr., is professor of law, Yale Law School, and an adjunct scholar at the American Enterprise Institute.

John R. Bolton is a member of the Yale Law School class of 1974 and an editor of the *Yale Law Journal*.

Domestic Affairs Study 19, October 1973

ISBN 0-8447-3118-8

Library of Congress Catalog Card No. L.C. 73-90059

Printed in United States of America

CONTENTS

CAMPAIGN FINANCING
AND POLITICAL FREEDOM

The conviction that something has gone awry in our political process is again growing stronger in the United States Congress. In particular, the view that wealth has excessive influence on election results and that election campaigns are too costly seems almost a routine assumption. These claims come on the heels of the Federal Election Campaign Act of 1971, a restrictive law regulating the contribution and use of campaign money. That act has been greeted by constitutional authorities with comments ranging from "would seem to violate the First Amendment" [1] to "flatly unconstitutional" [2] and has been challenged by lawyers for the *New York Times* as "shot through with constitutional deficiencies." [3] Hence considerable caution would seem warranted before federal regulation of campaign financing is expanded. Nevertheless, the Congress is seriously considering even more drastic legislation.

The principal proposals now under debate are relatively old and deceptively simple. In general outline they include a substantial subsidy from public funds to be given to federal candidates to pay all or part of their campaign costs. [4] This subsidy would be complemented by legal limits on (1) the amount spent by a candidate or those furthering a candidacy and (2) the size of individual financial contributions to a candidate's campaign.

---

[1] A. Rosenthal, *Federal Regulation of Campaign Finance: Some Constitutional Questions* (Princeton, N. J.: Citizens' Research Foundation (ed.), 1972), p. 63.

[2] Statement of Alexander Bickel, ibid., p. 66.

[3] Brief for *New York Times* as amicus curiae, p. 16, American Civil Liberties Union v. Jennings, Civil No. 1967-72 (D.D.C., 1972).

[4] See, for example, S. 1103, 93d Congress, 1st session (1973); hereinafter referred to as the Hart bill, after its author, Senator Hart.

Such proposals are of critical importance. If adopted, they will alter the political process and may have results transcending the issue of campaign financing. Moreover, because they regulate campaign advocacy, they may interfere with freedom of expression./

The proposals ought, therefore, to be implemented only after a persuasive demonstration of necessity and after a weighing of all potentially undesirable effects. The position taken here is that the case for further regulation, when scrutinized, seems based on speculation rather than demonstrated fact, ignores the grave dangers to a free society such regulation threatens, and emanates in part from groups which have political interests of their own to further.

1. Campaign Money in Perspective

The Functions of Private Campaign Money. Much of the doomsday rhetoric accompanying discussions of campaign finance can be discounted as political exaggeration. Candidates seem never to lose because the public is indifferent to them or to their platforms; they seem to lose because they cannot raise enough money. Tom Wicker tells us that Fred Harris and Paul McCloskey saw their campaigns founder "for want of means to wage a primary campaign," [5] a statement that is true in the same sense that if a mayoral candidate in New York City were exposed as Martin Bormann, his withdrawal statement would mention only difficulties in raising campaign funds.

Lack of campaign money provides a face-saving exit from a delicate (losing) situation. Thus, many attributed Senator Humphrey's loss in the California primary to Senator McGovern's money, and his loss to President Nixon to Nixon's money.

No one denies that elections are expensive, but the importance of money is almost universally exaggerated. Although allegations about the high campaign costs of recent years are repeatedly made, we really do not know how much was spent before the days of television when campaign expenditures were neither open nor easily regulable. Even now, the estimated amount spent for all elective offices in 1972, national, state and local, was less than was spent by each of two commercial advertisers.[6]

Still, since campaigns are expensive, large contributions seem an easy way to gain favor. Potential donors may be reminded of

---

[5] Tom Wicker, "Subsidizing Politics," *New York Times*, June 8, 1973, p. 39, col. 5.
[6] Statement of Herbert E. Alexander, *Hearings on S. 372 before the Subcommittee on Communications of the Senate Committee on Commerce*, 93d Congress, 1st session (1973), p. 219; hereinafter referred to as *Hearings*.

their dependence on governmental decisions by public officials or their representatives; some individuals give seemingly inordinate amounts; finally, continued allegations seem to have generated considerable skepticism about the financing of campaigns and to have eroded confidence in the political process.

Given all this, the case for regulation cannot be summarily dismissed, and the roles played by private campaign money must be carefully weighed. Certain functions *are* undesirable. Some donors doubtless make contributions hoping to obtain personal favors ranging from the trivial, for example, dinner invitations, to the malevolent. Awarding ambassadorships in return for large contributions is not the most desirable method of choosing American representatives to foreign nations. To exercise administrative discretion in favor of larger political contributors, for example, in awarding a government contract, is not only undesirable but in most cases illegal. Where the contribution follows a pointed reminder from a public official, governmental power is misused. Similarly, we feel uneasy when an otherwise undistinguished individual makes a serious stab at high office by expending a family fortune.

Horror stories illustrating the misuses of campaign money abound; but precisely because they horrify, they may obscure more than they illuminate. Many of the roles played by private campaign money are desirable, indeed, indispensable to a free and stable society.

Our threshold question must be whether money ought to play any role in politics. If we value freedom, the question can safely be answered affirmatively. All political activities make claims on society's resources. Speeches, advertisements, broadcasts, canvassing, and so on, all consume labor, newsprint, buildings, electrical equipment, transportation, and other resources. Money is a medium of exchange by which individuals employ resources to put to personal use, to work for others, or to devote to political purposes. If political activities are left to private financing, individuals are free to choose which activities to engage in, on behalf of which causes, or whether to do so at all. When the individual is deprived of this choice, either because government limits or prohibits his using money for political purposes or takes his money in taxes and subsidizes the political activities it chooses, his freedom is impaired.

The argument generally advanced in response is that money is so maldistributed that the political process is undesirably skewed. To foreshadow the conclusions below, it may briefly be said: first, because access to the resources most suitable for political use may be even more unevenly distributed than wealth, limitations solely on the use of money may aggravate rather than diminish the distortion; and second, money performs many valuable functions which far outweigh whatever harm it may do.

Candidates seeking change, for example, may have far greater need for, and make better use of, campaign money than those with established images or those defending the existing system. Money is, after all, subject to the law of diminishing returns and is of less use to the well known than to the newcomer. The existence of "seed money" may thus be an important agent of change. Both the Wallace campaigns and the antiwar candidacies achieved the significance they did largely because they raised and used "new" political money.

The solicitation and contribution of money also allow citizens who have little, or desire more, opportunity to participate meaningfully in the political process the chance to do so. Because of the obsession with horror stories, we forget that persons without much free time have few alternatives to contributions other than inaction.

Campaign contributions are also vehicles of expression for donors seeking to persuade other citizens on public issues. A contribution to a candidate holding convictions similar to the donor's employs the candidate as a surrogate for the expression of those ideas. Contributing to a candidate permits individuals to pool their resources and voice their message far more effectively than if each spoke singly. This is critically important because it permits citizens to join a potent organization and propagate their views beyond their voting districts. Persons who feel strongly about appointments to the Supreme Court, for example, can demonstrate their convictions by contributing to the campaigns of sympathetic congressmen. Those who give money to Mr. John Gardner's Common Cause and conceive of that act as a form of free association and expression should not automatically deny the same status to those who give to political campaigns.

Nor is there anything inherently wrong with contributing to candidates who agree with one's views on broad social and economic policies, even where those policies may benefit the donor. Obviously, groups pursue their self-interests and seek to persuade others to support them. That is a salient characteristic of a free political system. Persons who seek to regulate that kind of contribution can stand with those who would deny the vote to welfare recipients to prevent that vote from being "bought" by promises of higher benefits.

Many such contributions also represent broad interests that might otherwise be underrepresented. Suppose land developers mount a campaign against proposals to restrict the use of large undeveloped areas. Certainly they represent their own economic interests, but they also functionally represent potential purchasers, an interest group that would otherwise go unnoticed since few persons would consider themselves future purchasers.

These functions of campaign contributions are all too often ignored because critics of the present system mistake cause and effect. That a senator receives large union contributions might be perceived as the reason he often supports union causes. Is not the reverse far more commonly the case: the candidate receives contributions because he holds these convictions?

Contributions also serve as a barometer of the intensity of voter feeling. In a majoritarian system voters who feel exceptionally strongly about particular issues may be unable to reflect their feelings adequately in periodic votes.[7] As members of the antiwar movement often pointed out, the strength of their feelings as well as their numbers should have been taken into account. Indeed, if a substantial group feels intensely about an issue, a system which does not allow that feeling to be heard effectively may well be endangered. Campaign contributions are perhaps the most important means by which such intensity can be expressed. People who feel strongly about the defense of Israel, for example, are able to voice that conviction with greater effect through carefully directed campaign donations than in periodic elections in which the meaning of individual votes may be ambiguous.

This function might be discounted if large contributions reflected only intense but idiosyncratic views. For the most part, however, intense feelings will not generate substantial funds unless large numbers without great wealth also share those convictions. Campaign contributors in these circumstances serve as representatives or surrogates for the entire group. That Mr. X, who favors free trade, can make larger contributions than Mr. Y, who does not, really matters little, since Mr. Z agrees with Mr. Y and gives heavily.

Finally, the need for campaign money weeds out candidates who lack substantial public support. An attractive candidate with an attractive issue will draw money as well as votes. Money dries up because the candidate has little public support more often than public support dries up because the candidate has little money.[8] To avoid the anarchy of an overabundance of candidates, this function must be performed. Campaign contributions do just that and in a way that

---

[7] See, generally, Robert A. Dahl, *A Preface to Democratic Theory* (Chicago: University of Chicago Press, 1956).

[8] David A. Leuthold, *Electioneering in a Democracy: Campaigns for Congress* (New York: John Wiley and Sons, 1968), pp. 67-68.

roughly reflects voter support, or at least reflects it as well as any known alternative. Senator Harris could not raise funds because he had lost his political base in Oklahoma and was mining a political vein already being worked by Senator McGovern. And Congressman McCloskey's campaign was an attempt to capitalize on one issue rather than a serious bid for the nomination.

Private Campaign Money: Where Is the Balance? Does the available evidence support the claims that the undesirable functions of private campaign money outweigh the desirable? If so, does that evidence call for regulation of the breadth and scope being suggested? To both these questions, the answer is no.

The strongest case for the proponents of regulation is that of money being used to gain personal favor through the exercise of executive discretion. But even with full credit given to all the allegations, the call for over-arching restrictive laws cannot be justified. Ambassadorships, for instance, are subject to a veto by the very same Senate that seeks to regulate campaign financing. Similarly, if government contracts are being awarded to large campaign contributors, the irresistible conclusion is that it is the process of determining awards that is fundamentally wrong. Ending the use of private money will not eliminate political influence. Contracts will simply be awarded to those displaying political loyalty in other ways.

Where the candidacies of the rich are concerned, the allegations about wealth also contain truth but are of inconclusive impact. Otherwise, one must conclude that the political careers of Nelson Rockefeller and the Kennedys, for example, are illegitimate, a conclusion from which one ought to shy because their political success is so obviously based on more than wealth. The allegations fail in not demonstrating a net harm to the system. Of course, wealth aids a candidate in a way that seems unfair. But if the influence of campaign money were eliminated, even more irrational factors, for example, the media exposure which falls to astronauts and sportscasters (Senator Cosell?), might become more significant. Nor is there evidence that the political behavior of office holders with personal wealth differs greatly from that of those without.

In any event, where wealth alone generates the candidacy, the evidence does not support the more extreme charges. Two recent candidacies alleged to be wholly based on personal wealth—those of Mr. Metzenbaum of Ohio and Mr. Ottinger of New York—failed in the general election. (Had Mr. Metzenbaum not run, the Democratic candidate would have been John Glenn.) If campaign money is so important an issue, persons running against the wealthy can use it to their advantage.

No one seriously contends that money has been decisive in presidential elections.[9] Of course, candidates of third parties raise less money, but that is to be expected because of their weakness at the polls and not because fringe movements are wholly unable to raise funds. History is replete with movements which began at the fringe of American politics and, because they raised salient issues, were able to attract funds and, over time, to affect the course of American history. Consider the achievements of the NAACP Legal Defense Fund. (Not to mention the money-raising ability of the Black Panthers.)[10] And once such movements take hold, candidates representing their points of view get campaign money.

---

[9] The Democratic Party, for instance, elected Presidents from 1932 to 1952, but spent less money than the Republicans. In more recent years, John Kennedy spent his party into debt in 1960, but that may well have been necessary to overcome what was at that time a religious disability. As one scholar computed 1960 spending, "the 1960 ratio of Democratic to Republican spending appears to have been almost as close as the 1960 election returns." See Herbert E. Alexander, *Financing the 1960 Election* (Princeton, N. J.: Citizens' Research Foundation, 1961), pp. 9-11. In 1964 Barry Goldwater considerably broadened the Republican Party's financial base and outspent his Democratic opponent. Nevertheless, the best-financed and most narrowly based Democratic campaign in history to that point, plus the advantages of incumbency, more than outweighed Goldwater's mass contributions. See ibid., pp. 7-16. The Goldwater campaign (and, to a lesser extent, the McGovern campaign) demonstrate an interesting interrelationship of two themes in the text: (1) campaign money tends to go to winners, and (2) intensely held feelings generate funds supporting those feelings. Although Goldwater and McGovern consistently showed poorly in the public opinion polls, the strong philosophical convictions of their supporters nonetheless generated considerable amounts of money, especially in relatively small donations. The Nixon 1972 victory repeated the 1960 pattern: contributions mirrored almost exactly the eventual popular vote totals of the two major candidates. Although both Goldwater and McGovern were swamped on election day, they at least had an opportunity to voice the strongly held feelings of their ardent supporters. That they did so against strongly entrenched incumbent Presidents and that two men of such differing political persuasions could become nominees of the two major parties only eight years apart is an amazing testimony to the freedom and stability of American politics. The only apparent exception to the proposition in the text accompanying this footnote is the 1968 election. Republicans outspent Democrats in the general election campaign, but the Democrats exceeded Republican outlays in the pre-conventions struggles for the nomination. The political reality of 1968 thus explains the Democrats' inability to raise money: the party began in debt and was deeply and acrimoniously split; it ended in even greater debt and with internal turmoil still unresolved. (Ibid.)

[10] See Tom Wolfe, "Radical Chic," in *Radical Chic and Mau-Mauing the Flak Catchers* (New York: Farrar, Straus and Giroux, 1970).

The role of the rich patron in bringing about change should not be ignored. As Milton Friedman has noted:

> Radical movements . . . have typically been supported by a few wealthy individuals who have become persuaded—by a Frederick Vanderbilt Field, or an Anita McCormick Blaine, or a Corliss Lamont, to mention a few names recently prominent, or by a Friedrich Engels, to go farther back. This is a role of inequality of wealth in preserving political freedom that is seldom noted—the role of the patron.[11]

Many of the allegations about money blocking social change quite simply ignore history. During the last forty years, an immense amount of social and regulatory legislation has been enacted, this alone refuting the assertion that campaign money is a barrier to change. That the charges come so hard upon the extensive legislation of the Great Society and from the very architects of those programs seems particularly inappropriate.[12]

For all the heat generated by allegations about private campaign money, there is no body of settled scholarship to support them. No one denies that contributions sometimes play an undesirable or even corrupting role. But no system is without friction and, where the system involves money, whether it be taxation, welfare or campaign contributions, there will be abuses. Contrary to the allegations so widely heard, however, serious scholars are generally in agreement that money is only one factor influencing elections and that its impact is not, on balance, either decisive or harmful.

In response to the rhetorical question, "Does money win?" Dr. Herbert E. Alexander of the Citizens' Research Foundation, for example, answered that money is the "common denominator helping to shape the factors that make for electoral success. . . ."[13] He agreed that certain minimal amounts are probably necessary, but noted that "little is known of the marginal increment per dollar or of the differential effectiveness of the various campaign techniques."[14] Among

---

[11] Milton Friedman, *Capitalism and Freedom* (Chicago: University of Chicago Press, 1962), p. 17.

[12] The inconclusive results of the social programs of the 1960s may be a cause of the present flap over campaign financing. Frustrated over the failure of these programs to produce the expected results, their proponents may automatically assume that something must be wrong with the political process.

[13] Herbert E. Alexander, "Links and Contrasts Among American Parties and Party Subsystems," in Arnold J. Heidenheimer, ed., *Comparative Political Finance: The Financing of Party Organizations and Election Campaigns* (Indianapolis: Heath, D. C. and Co., 1970), p. 104.

[14] Ibid., p. 103.

other possibly determining factors, Alexander listed the predisposition of voters, the issues, group support, incumbency, chances for electoral victory, sympathy on the part of the mass media, and a collection of other factors (religion, divorce, and color).[15] On another occasion, Dr. Alexander testified:

> . . . it is well to remember that the availability of money for a given campaign may be an inherent effect of our democratic and pluralistic system—either the constitutional right to spend one's own money or to financially support candidates with congenial viewpoints or a manifestation of popularity. This is not to say that monied interests do not sometimes take advantage of a candidate's need for funds, or that candidates do not sometimes become beholden to special interests. They do, but that is part of the price we pay for a democratic system in which political party discipline is lacking and the candidate (and some of the public) may value his independence from the party.[16]

David Adamany reached essentially the same conclusions when he argued that "primarily, the patterns of campaign finance are a response to the political environment; but it is also true that the relationship is reciprocal inasmuch as the uses of money may, within very significant limits, shape the political system." [17] The programmatic orientation of parties and candidates is the resource Adamany deems most important, followed by personal charisma, finance organization, incumbency, and several others.[18] Unlike many of the reform advocates, he believes that:

> . . . a sophisticated examination shows that by most measures Americans pay a small cost for the maintenance of an adversary political process in a complicated federal system with its many elective offices at a variety of levels of government. . . . Even the scholarly work on campaign finance tends to concentrate on the amounts spent, the sources from which the money is raised, and the uses to which the money is put. These data are all helpful, but they do not show the relationship of campaign finance to the political environment— to the kinds of party systems, the available channels of com-

---

[15] Ibid., pp. 103-104.

[16] Statement of Dr. Herbert E. Alexander in *Hearings*, p. 224.

[17] David Adamany, *Financing Politics: Recent Wisconsin Elections* (Madison: University of Wisconsin Press, 1969), p. 230.

[18] Ibid., pp. 231-233.

munication, and other political and social phenomena. Nor is money ordinarily viewed as a form of functional representation by groups in the community and as just one of the several ways in which groups may seek their policy objectives through the allocation of resources to the political process. . . . Yet much less attention is given to money as a form of functional representation than to the very infrequent instances in which campaign gifts are made for the purpose of procuring actions by public officials which would not have been forthcoming in the absence of contributions.[19]

Alexander Heard, in his classic work on campaign finance, *The Costs of Democracy*, has concluded:

> And it has been repeatedly demonstrated that he who pays the piper does *not* always call the tune, at least not in politics. Politicians prize votes more than dollars.
> Contrary to frequent assertions, American campaign monies are *not* supplied solely by a small handful of fat cats. Many millions of people now give to politics. Even those who give several hundred dollars each number in the tens of thousands.
> And the traditional fat cats are *not* all of one species, allied against common adversaries. Big givers show up importantly in both parties and on behalf of many opposing candidates.[20]

Finally, the much respected political scientist V. O. Key has noted:

> Considerable analysis has been made of the sources of contributions to national committees. The findings, in essence, seem to be that each party draws heavily on those elements of society traditionally associated with it. . . . The cynical view that a campaign contribution is equivalent to a bribe at times indubitably matches the facts. Yet the significance of money in politics can be grasped only by a view that places party finance in the total context of the political process. . . . That the unbridled dominance of money would run counter to the tenets of a democratic order may be indisputable. On the other hand, a democratic regime that tyrannized men of wealth would both commit injustice and perhaps destroy its instruments of production.[21]

---

[19] Ibid., p. 244.

[20] Alexander Heard, *The Costs of Democracy* (Chapel Hill: University of North Carolina Press, 1960), p. 6.

[21] V. O. Key, Jr., *Politics, Parties, and Pressure Groups*, 5th ed. (New York: T. Y. Crowell, 1964), pp. 495, 513.

In the face of this scholarship, perhaps in studied ignorance of it, stand the unsupported and impressionistic assertions of groups such as Common Cause and the National Committee for an Effective Congress. Common Cause, we are told, is presently engaged in an empirical study designed to show "a real correlation" [22] between contributions and legislative decisions. There should be little doubt that such a correlation will be discovered, for two reasons. Common Cause, after all, first made up its mind and is just now studying the evidence. Given that, it would be foolhardy to anticipate findings that disputed its earlier judgment. In any event, some such correlation can probably be easily established, since contributions are rarely given either at random or to one's political enemies.

Existing scholarship is thus at odds with the charges that advocates of regulation make. In the absence of evidence to support these charges, caution in treading this dangerous political terrain seems the prudent course. Some day this evidence may come into being, but there will be time enough then to tamper with our freedoms.

Two other considerations deserve mention. First, limiting the use of private money in election campaigns will hardly decrease the influence of affluent people, for direct access to resources easily converted to political purposes is concentrated among various sectors of the well-to-do. While the power of those who rely on contributions will decline, that of at least three groups in society will be increased: (1) pressure groups which operate "issue" (rather than "political") campaigns, (2) political activists with free time, and (3) those who control the media. All three, however, represent wealth in one form or another.

Most interest organizations such as Common Cause and the American Medical Association (AMA) necessarily rely on large amounts of money and generally have an affluent constituency.[23] (Common Cause spent $847,856 on lobbying in 1971; the AMA spent

---

[22] Walter Pincus, "Raising the Money to Run," *The New Republic*, vol. 169, no. 12 (September 29, 1973), p. 16.

[23] Unions represent a constituency certainly less affluent than that of Common Cause and the AMA. Nonetheless, unions are wealthier than many other interest groups and, because of union security clauses, can raise money very efficiently. Moreover, unions compensate for any relative lack of funds in two ways: (1) American unions have generally limited the focus of their activities to issues which affect only the interests of their membership, in contrast to European unions, and (2) in light of the first point, union leaders have become highly skilled political technicians, developing an expertise perhaps unequalled among lobbying groups.

$114,800.) [24] It may be more than coincidence, therefore, that Common Cause, a pressure group representing relatively affluent political activists and students, has adopted this issue as its own. Moreover, an individual cannot spend a great deal of time leading movements to "dump the President" without access to wealth. Restrictions on the use of private money will also increase dependence for exposure on the goodwill of those who control the media.

Much of this is admittedly speculative, but as long as proposals for regulating campaign money are seriously advanced, such speculation is necessary. Interestingly enough, though, many of those in the forefront of the battle for regulation are in fact affluent and influential, rather than poor and powerless. Such ostensible self-abnegation deserves the same scrutiny as is given to large contributions to political campaigns.

Finally, all of the allegations about the influence of money reflect a basic and disturbing mistrust of the people. If campaign financing really "distorts" legislative or executive behavior, candidates can raise its effect as an issue and the voters can respond at election time. The call for legislation thus seems based on the belief that the voters cannot be relied upon to perceive their own best interests.

Moreover, if one really believes the people are easily fooled and so in need of protection, there is no end to the campaign tactics eligible for regulation and no end to the need to increase the power of those *not* fooling the public. Indeed, the most disquieting aspect of the drive to regulate campaign money is that so many of its adherents view themselves as possessing a monopoly of political truth. Thus, many of the allegations about the influence of money are based on nothing more than the fact that some pet program has not yet been approved by Congress, a fact which the supporters of those programs can explain only by corruption.[25] Since they alone act in the "public interest," moreover, they all too often see little need for permitting their opponents, who always pursue selfish interests, to further their vision of the truth. Consider the remarks of a representative of the National Committee for an Effective Congress when confronted with the argument that its spending, as well as that of other groups, might be subject to legislative control. "I'm for putting us [NCEC] out of business," she said, "I think it's the only answer. The public interest groups know they can never match the amount vested interests can give. Why preserve the right to give when you know you will be at

---

[24] "Lobby Spending: Common Cause Leads Again," *Congressional Quarterly*, June 9, 1973, p. 1425.
[25] Pincus, "Raising the Money to Run," p. 17.

a disadvantage?" [26] For that matter, why preserve the right to speak when you know you will not persuade?

2. Campaign Financing and the Law

A number of general considerations apply to all regulation of campaign financing and deserve independent discussion. First, regulation must be enacted by those in power and the desire to maintain and increase that power will not be suspended while the legislation is being considered. How those who allege that campaign money has such a corrupting effect on legislators can expect those same legislators to enact "neutral" regulations on its use is one of the great mysteries of the present debate.

The influence of self-interest on legislation regulating political financing is everywhere to be seen by those who care to look. Even Common Cause is, Pandora-like, worried that low limits on expenditures for House of Representatives races will protect incumbents.[27] And what applies to the House surely applies to every political office.

There are, moreover, inconsistencies in the 1971 law which can only be explained by political considerations. The amount a senatorial candidate can spend in a state, say New York, is limited, presumably to prevent one candidate from overwhelming his opponent with a "media blitz." Limitations on spending by presidential candidates, however, apply nationally, rather than state by state. Since presidential elections are determined by the electoral votes of the states, not the national popular vote, consistency would call for spending limits state by state. Otherwise a candidate might take money properly allocated to, say, southern and southwestern states to finance a "blitz" in New York. That the consistent route was not chosen doubtless was due to uncertainty as to which party would be helped, or, perhaps, to the conviction that it would be the "wrong" party.

Finally, everyone agrees that incumbents get an unfair advantage from governmental subsidies such as offices, the frank, paid staffs, and so on. Removing these advantages, or, in the alternative, giving challengers an offsetting subsidy, can be justified. Yet such legislation is politically impossible. That fact alone casts the shadow of suspicion over any measure that can pass.

Free societies must shun regulation of political speech which claims to eliminate "distortions" or to protect the public from being

---

26 "Financing Campaigns: Growing Pressure for Reform," *Congressional Quarterly*, July 14, 1973, p. 1880.
27 *Common Cause Report from Washington*, vol. 3, no. 9 (September 1973), p. 2.

fooled. No one has a monopoly on political truth and the claim that laws are needed to "correct" [28] the electoral process by regulating campaign advocacy should be viewed with alarm, particularly when those laws are passed by such interested parties. Mr. Justice Holmes once said, in a justly famous passage:

> But when men have realized that time has upset many fighting faiths they may come to believe even more than they believe the very foundations of their own conduct that the ultimate good desired is better reached by free trade in ideas —that the best test of truth is the power of the thought to get itself accepted in the competition of the market. . . .[29]

Those who would regulate campaign advocacy should ponder Mr. Holmes's view of freedom of expression and his spirit of tolerance, for it is the complete answer to the question—"Why preserve the right to give when you know you will be at a disadvantage?"

Because all such legislation intrudes on freedom of expression, constitutional precedent requires that it be carefully tailored to the harm it seeks to cure and not be overly broad. Thus where "less drastic" measures are available to achieve the congressional objective, the courts will invalidate a statute which encroaches on individual liberties.[30] Many of the proposals now under consideration seem infected by over-breadth, for they lump all contributions together, making no distinctions as to their sources or kinds.[31]

If ambassadorships are given in return for large campaign contributions, the Senate can refuse to confirm. If government contracts are now awarded on the basis of politics, they will continue to be so awarded whether or not there are campaign contributors. All the

---

[28] See statement of Russell D. Hemenway, national director, National Committee for an Effective Congress, in *Hearings*, p. 165.

[29] Abrams v. United States, 250 U.S. 616, 630 (Holmes, J., dissenting).

[30] In Aptheker v. Secretary of State, 378 U.S. 500 (1964), the Supreme Court declared unconstitutional Section 6 of the Subversive Activities Control Act of 1950, 50 U.S.C. Section 785. That statute denied to any member of a registered Communist organization (or one ordered to be registered) the right to apply for a passport, or the renewal of one, or to attempt to use any such passport, knowing of the registration. The Court, in an opinion by Justice Goldberg, noted that "in determining the constitutionality of Section 6, it is also important to consider that Congress has within its power 'less drastic' means of achieving the congressional objective of safeguarding our national security. . . . The section judged by its plain import and by the substantive evil which Congress sought to control, sweeps too widely and too indiscriminately across the liberty guaranteed by the First Amendment. . . . here, as elsewhere, precision must be the touchstone of legislation so affecting basic freedoms." 378 U.S. 500, 512-514.

[31] For example, all contributions over $100 must be disclosed. See p. 21.

allegations about contracts and contributions prove is that we need laws limiting official discretion in this area.

Those who would regulate political financing should also look to reducing superfluous economic regulation. If milk producers make contributions in return for higher price supports, why should not this subsidy and all similar programs be repealed? It is no answer to say that well-placed contributions make repeal politically impossible, since that argument applies with more convincing force to legislation forbidding contributions. "Big government" vastly increases the power of public officials to give and take away and thus creates undesirable appearances as well as temptations. It. never occurs to those who would regulate campaign financing that perhaps a more direct remedy would be to reduce the amount of unnecessary economic regulation. Oft times, in fact, they seem to regard that as a fate worse than death.

In addition, regulating campaign financing through the criminal law necessarily contemplates trials of political figures after elections. The danger in this, one hopes, is evident to all, for prosecutions are all too subject to political influence and all too effective a means of silencing one's opponents. The danger is not the less because present law contains so many complex requirements and contemplates such extensive bookkeeping that violations are all but unavoidable.

Furthermore, all regulation of campaign financing is based on an irrational distinction. No fully rational line separates election campaigns from all of the political and propaganda activities which occur between elections. If money is all that powerful a deceiver, it will work its evil ways between campaigns as well as during them. If spending by a candidate's election committee can be regulated, why not spending by organizations like the Committee on Political Education (COPE) or some in the Nader group. After all, *The New Republic* raised the question of the propriety of Nader's Center for Auto Safety taking money from the American Trial Lawyers Association when he and the association were silent on the no-fault issue.[32] Indeed, Mr. John Gardner himself, not to mention the representative of the National Committee for an Effective Congress quoted above, is reported to have urged the abolition of COPE.[33]

Business and union groups, for example, are irrationally forced to distinguish between "political" activities (during the campaign)

---

[32] Leah Young, "A Chink in Nader's Armor?" *The New Republic*, vol. 167, no. 8 (September 2, 1972), p. 11.

[33] "Witnesses Debate Campaign Funds," *Washington Post*, December 6, 1972, reprinted in *Hearings*, p. 376.

and "educational" activities (during the interim). The only functional distinction between the periods is that the activities in the former tend to focus on particular candidates. Candidates are often known well in advance and activities designed to influence their election go on for months before the formal campaign. Consider the following passage, which happens to be discussing the activities of COPE, but which is equally applicable to business and other organizations:

> Federal law requires COPE to draw a line between its political and educational activities, but in practice the distinction is difficult to maintain. . . . The educational activities of COPE embrace a wide variety of programs, including voter registration drives, organization of local and state COPE units, news releases to union journals, posters and exhibits. Most of the money, however, is spent on preparation and distribution of informational pamphlets on political issues and candidates' voting records. In 1956, COPE distributed 30 million pieces of literature, including 10.2 million copies of its voting record on members of Congress. In 1957, an off-year, some 7 million pieces were distributed.
>
> As a practical matter, COPE officials say that anything short of a direct appeal to "Vote for Candidate X" can be included in the category of educational activities.
>
> A few examples will show how thin is the line, in practice, between education and partisan politics:
>
> Registration drives—obviously the necessary first step to any successful political action, are non-partisan in nature, hence educational.
>
> Pamphlets on political issues—current ones, include broadsides on farm policies, unemployment, the budget, taxes, social security, school legislation—are educational, even when they contain such partisan references as "Mr. Eisenhower's Big Business Administration."
>
> Voting records—in which members of Congress are scored as being "right" or "wrong" on selected roll calls involving many of these same issues, are educational, even though the implications are obviously partisan. . . .
>
> The same distinction is applied to COPE personnel. One COPE officer told CQ that part of his own salary is switched from the educational account to the political account after a certain date in each campaign year.[34]

Laws regulating campaign financing, therefore, compel accounting distinctions without political significance. The statistics reflecting

---

[34] *Congressional Quarterly*, March 28, 1958, pp. 384-386.

what money was spent for "political purposes" are, moreover, wholly inaccurate since they do not include "educational" expenses or the fixed amounts of maintaining an organization which, with little effort, turns to campaign work when the time comes.

Limitations on Expenditures and Contributions: Price Controls in the Marketplace of Ideas. These limitations fall into two categories.

(1) *Limits on Spending by Candidates.* Those who seek to impose limits on expenditures by candidates face a dilemma of constitutional dimensions. On the one hand, if the limitation applies only to expenditures explicitly authorized by the candidate, it will be, in Lyndon Johnson's famous phrase, "more loophole than law." "Independent" committees will carry on the campaign. On the other hand, if it seeks to charge the candidate with all outlays (from whatever source) that further his candidacy, it must give the candidate a veto over the actions of all those who would support him through monetary expenditures. The campaign reform law of 1971 thus prohibits the media from charging for political advertising unless the candidate certifies that the charge will not cause his spending to exceed the limit.[35] The effect, therefore, is to restrict the freedom of individuals to buy advertising supporting or, under the regulations promulgated by the Comptroller General of the United States,[36] attacking, in some circumstances, a candidate.

Indeed, in light of decisions of the Supreme Court, there would hardly seem reason to debate the issue at length. In *New*

---

[35] 47 U.S.C. Section 803(b) states that "No person may make any charge for the use by or on behalf of any legally qualified candidate for Federal elective office (or for nomination to such office) of any newspaper, magazine, or outdoor advertising facility, unless such candidate (or a person specifically authorized by such candidate in writing to do so) certifies in writing to the person making such charge that the payment of such charge will not violate paragraph (1), (2), or (3) of subsection (a) of this section, whichever is applicable."

[36] 11 C.F.R., Section 4.5 states that: "Section 4.5: Amounts spent urging candidate's defeat or derogating his stand. (a) An expenditure for the use of communications media opposing or urging the defeat of a Federal candidate, or derogating his stand on campaign issues, shall not be deemed to be an expenditure for the use of communications media on behalf of any other Federal candidate and shall not be charged against any other Federal candidate's applicable expenditure limitation under section 104(a) of the Act and this part, unless such other Federal candidate has directly or indirectly authorized such use or unless the circumstances of such use taken as a whole are such that consent may reasonably be imputed to such other candidate."

What may or may not be "reasonably imputed to such other candidate" is not described with any specificity.

York Times v. *Sullivan*,[37] the Court held that a newspaper advertisement on public issues was entitled to First Amendment protection. The fact that the *New York Times* was paid for the advertisement was "immaterial."[38] In *Eastern Richmond President's Conference* v. *Noerr Motor Freight*,[39] moreover, the Court held that the Sherman Act did not apply to advertisements intended to influence legislation specifically designed to injure competitors. In that case, certain railroad companies had conducted a publicity campaign which was "vicious, corrupt, and fraudulent" and "designed to foster the adoption and retention of laws and law enforcement practices destructive of the trucking business. . . ."[40] Rejecting the claim that such activities violated the Sherman Act, the Supreme Court, through Mr. Justice Black, stated,

> It is neither unusual nor illegal for people to seek action on laws in the hope that they may bring about an advantage to themselves and a disadvantage to their competitors. . . . [T]o disqualify people from taking a public position in matters in which they are financially interested would thus deprive the government of a valuable source of information and . . . deprive the people of their right to petition in the very instances in which that right may be of the most importance to them.[41]

The entire theory of the decision, therefore, rests on the First Amendment policy of protecting groups in their efforts to influence government to act in their interests. Moreover, the efforts in this case, namely, the financing of a systematic publicity campaign designed to induce favorable governmental action, are of particular relevance to this discussion. If Congress cannot stop individuals from conducting the kind of campaigns that were involved in *Noerr*, surely it may not do so when the issue is the election of an individual to office.

The First Amendment has given rise to considerable disagreement as to its scope. All agree, however, that it protects political speech. If we are to have "free trade in ideas" in the political sphere, individual citizens must be free to express whatever ideas they choose in whatever form they believe appropriate, whether or not it costs them money. There is no room for price controls in the marketplace of ideas.

---

[37] 376 U.S. 254 (1964).
[38] Ibid., p. 266.
[39] 365 U.S. 126 (1961).
[40] Ibid., p. 129.
[41] Ibid., p. 127.

Setting a limit on candidate expenditures sets a maximum on the political activities in which American citizens can engage and is thus unconstitutional. The reasoning that speech which costs money is too persuasive cannot be contained. For one can also argue that demonstrations of more than a certain number of people, extensive voter canvassing, or too many billboards with catchy slogans also "distort" public opinion and also ought to be regulated.

The freedom to speak is not the only liberty infringed by such legislation. Because giving to a candidate permits individuals to "pool" their contributions and act as part of an effective organization, limitations on candidate spending are in effect restrictions on the freedom of association.

Furthermore, effective limits on expenditures must help incumbents, who have an established image and all the advantages of known quantities over unknown. To limit campaign spending is to limit what a challenger can do to offset these advantages.[42] That the first effective regulation approved by Congress was a limit on spending should be pondered long and hard by those supporting further legislation of this kind.

Finally, a truly effective limit on spending is not feasible. Many expenditures are individually too small to be controlled when private citizens make them—for example, buttons, bumper stickers, carfare for canvassers. In the aggregate, however, they may entail a significant amount which, because they are not regulable, would permit money to continue to "distort" elections even after extensive regulations have been enacted. Candidates would, moreover, be encouraged to emphasize such activities since they would be in effect free from restrictions. The laws we pass, therefore, may control only that which is regulable simply because it is regulable, not because the desired end, limiting the impact of money, will be achieved.

(2) *Limits on Individual Contributions.* Except where someone seeks personal gain in direct exchange for a campaign contribution, individual donations are political activities. Limitations on their size are thus an explicit restriction on political freedom. If a person feels strongly about the defense of Israel, the conduct of the Indochina War, or the continuation of farm subsidies, why should he not have the right to finance appropriate political activities, whether or not (or, particularly if) those activities are part of a political campaign?

---

[42] See Lester G. Telser, "Advertising and Competition," *Journal of Political Economy,* December 1964, p. 537, which finds that advertising is most effective in introducing new products.

Again, government regulation establishes a dangerous precedent. If one can limit the size of individual contributions, why cannot (or, should not) the government limit the extent of voluntary activity on behalf of candidates? Both involve giving a thing of value to a candidate, and both are designed to further his candidacy. Both, moreover, create "obligations." The only distinction is between the use of time and ability directly for the candidate and the use of income gained through the expenditure of time and ability. These activities are largely fungible, a fact that Congress recognized when it specifically excepted volunteer services from the definition of "contribution" in the 1971 statute.[43]

Again, associational rights are involved since a limit on the size of one's contribution limits one's ability to "pool" resources with others. Indeed, there is a practical risk in limiting the size of individual contributions. If the Supreme Court were to strike down the candidate's veto over individual spending but uphold a low limit on contributions to candidates, the effect would be the opposite of that intended. The wealthy would be able to conduct their independent advertising campaigns while everyone else would be limited in their ability to pool resources behind a candidate.

Reporting and Disclosure Legislation. Laws of this kind in effect require that political acts of individuals be registered with the government and publicized. Such legislation thus might subject potential contributors to the fear that persons with different views or political affiliations, for example, clients, employers, officials who award government contracts, might retaliate. The effect, therefore, might be to "chill" or deter political activity, a result with First Amendment implications.

This constitutional issue falls within a growing class of cases in which persons or organizations claim a right to anonymity. Newsmen thus claim a privilege not to disclose sources, the NAACP has resisted the efforts of southern states to compel disclosure of its membership lists, and many say a state may not require that those who distribute handbills reveal the author or sponsor. Because there is no absolute right to anonymity, these claims have met with varying success in the Supreme Court.[44] What is involved is a weighing of the claimed need for disclosure against the deterrent effect publicity may have on the exercise of individual rights.

---

[43] 18 U.S.C., Section 591(e)(5).

[44] See, for example, Bates v. Little Rock, 361 U.S. 516, 524 (1960); Talley v. California, 362 U.S. 60 (1960); and U.S. v. Caldwell, 408 U.S. 665 (1972).

Reporting and disclosure statutes are generally said to rest on the need to let the public determine whether official conduct is being swayed by contributors in undesirable ways. Existing laws cannot be justified on that basis, however. For example, disclosure is required of every contribution of $100 or more to a presidential campaign.[45] Yet it is flatly unbelievable that a contribution of that size could have an undesirable impact. The law thus seems overly broad and subject to constitutional challenge.

To the extent that disclosure laws focus on contributions from those doing business with the government and on large contributions, the constitutional claims against them lose their force. To the extent that they forbid anonymity across the board to all contributors, however, the conclusion that the deterrent effect outweighs the need seems irresistible.

The Case against Public Financing. Most of the proposals for public financing of political campaigns include limitations on candidate expenditures and individual contributions.[46] To the extent that the subsidy and the limitations complement each other rather than exist independently, the case for subsidies is weaker. To the extent that the subsidy is not conditioned on limits on expenditures and contributions and is designed to aid candidates challenging incumbents by offsetting the financial advantages of incumbency, the case is stronger. Most subsidy proposals, however, do more than offset the financial advantages of incumbency.

(1) *Some Myths About Public Financing.* One allegation about providing financial subsidies to political candidates is that the temptation to engage in illegal activities would diminish.[47] Both experience and logic suggest this would not be the case. Experience with subsidies in Puerto Rico demonstrates that the subsidies are used up before the election and that the illegal solicitation of funds, for example, from government employees, ensues.[48] Such a result seems logical, for there is no fixed amount needed for a truly contested campaign. It is a myth to think that the provision of subsidies would change this. In fact, activities such as the Watergate break-in are more likely to occur in campaigns where the level of normal propa-

---

[45] 2 U.S.C., Sections 431-434.

[46] See, for example, the Hart bill, Sections 11-14.

[47] See TV address of Spiro T. Agnew, *New York Times*, October 16, 1973, p. 34.

[48] Henry Wells and Robert Anderson, *Government Financing of Political Parties in Puerto Rico: A Supplement to Study Number Four* (Princeton, N. J.: Citizens' Research Foundation, 1966), p. 5.

ganda is low than in campaigns where extensive activities of the ordinary kind take place. The argument that we can reduce the number of break-ins by limiting the amount of advertising on television and by financing campaigns with public money seems a dramatic non sequitur.

A second allegation made on behalf of subsidies is that they would increase "the opportunities for meaningful participation in . . . electoral contests without regard to the financial resources available to individual candiates. . . ."[49] But how many would become candidates if we subsidized campaigns? Unrestricted access to such subsidies would be an incentive to everyone with a yen for publicity to become a candidate; elections would thus become an anarchic jungle with policy issues wholly obscured. For that reason, many subsidy proposals suggest limitations on eligibility. One formula might call for a subsidy adjusted to performance on previous elections, but that seems unfair to newcomers and overly generous to the "old guard." Another route would be to adjust the subsidy according to performance in the election itself. For example, the Hart bill (which applies only to Senate and House races but could easily be extended to presidential campaigns) would require a security deposit equal to one-fifth of the anticipated subsidy. If the candidate got less than 10 percent of the total vote, the deposit would be forfeited. If he got less than 5 percent, he would have to repay whatever subsidy he had received.[50]

Such a provision, however, is hardly consistent with the bill's ostensible purpose. A candidate such as Fred Harris, for example, might well have no chance under such a law. If he refused the subsidy, it would be a signal that he did not take his chances seriously. He would then be quite unlikely to raise substantial funds, unless he had a rich patron, an alternative closed off by limits on individual contributions. If he took the subsidy, he would risk bankruptcy. The Hart formula could thus be a Trojan horse to the average candidate.

What the formula would create, however, would be a temptation for those who anticipated financial gain from running for office. Under the Hart plan, the author/candidate might be encouraged to enter the race to gather material for a book. A publisher's advance could cover the cost of posting the security bond or returning the subsidy. Similarly, many young lawyers would be likely to find it profitable to enter congressional races and take their chances on the

---

[49] Hart bill, Section 2(1).
[50] Ibid., Section 7(a).

subsidy in order to get publicity beneficial to their practices. Even if they might have to forfeit their bond or return the subsidy, it might seem a good risk when the amount was capitalized over the period of time that the anticipated income would accrue. The Hart formula might thus increase the number of non-serious candidates while discouraging those the bill is designed to aid.

Third, subsidies, it is said, will "prevent the relatively few individuals who have access to a great wealth from having an excessive influence upon the presentation of competing viewpoints . . . and from preempting the channels of mass communication as candidates or as contributors. . . ." [51] To be sure, subsidies combined with limits on contributions might exclude some people who are presently influential. But it does not follow that the number with effective influence would be increased. Those affluent people using free time in politics would become more powerful, as would those controlling the media. It is simply illogical to believe that taking power from one group will increase the power of those who presently lack it. Quite the contrary, power might well be concentrated in a smaller and more narrow group.

Fourth, it is alleged that public financing will help determine "the extent to which expenditure levels may be substantially higher than necessary for the conduct of a competitive, informative, and effective campaign. . . ." [52] This statement, too, seems a non sequitur, since a subsidy tells us nothing about whether present non-subsidized expenditures are excessive. In addition, provision of a subsidy would almost surely increase the amounts spent, as it did in Puerto Rico. [53]

Finally, we are told that subsidies will "reduce the pressure on Congressional candidates for dependence on large campaign contributions from private sources. . . ." [54] If, however, one reduces the pressure on candidates to look to the views of contributors, to whom will the candidates look instead? The need to raise money compels candidates to address those matters about which large groups feel strongly. Candidates might well, upon receiving campaign money from the government, mute their views and become even more prepackaged. Eliminate the need for money and you eliminate much of the motive to face up to the issues. Candidates might then look more

[51] Ibid., Section 2(2).

[52] Ibid., Section 2(3).

[53] Arlen J. Large, "How Should We Finance Elections?" *Wall Street Journal*, May 10, 1973, p. 24, col. 4.

[54] Hart bill, Section 2(4).

to attention-getting gimmicks than to attention-getting policy statements. A subsidy combined with spending limits might insulate incumbents both from challengers and the strongly held desires of constituents.

(2) *The Dangers in Public Financing.* Subsidy plans are not well conceived either as to need or impact. They are a classic case of tactics overwhelming the strategic issue, with many proponents of public financing more concerned with getting the principle accepted than with working out the "details." But attention to the details shows the principle to be erroneous, for not only are the claims made on behalf of subsidies empty, but such proposals also seem dangerous.

The use of private money is said to have weakened public confidence in the democratic process. We ought to ask, however, whether confidence is likely to be restored when taxpayers pay for campaigns they regard as frivolous, wasteful, and, in some cases, abhorrent. Would the taxpayer viewing television spots have more confidence because part of the tab came out of his paycheck? Would the voter have more confidence because he had to help pay for activities with which he disagreed? What would happen if a racist ran for office and delivered radical and quasi-violent speeches? One result might be cries for even more regulation—in particular, for regulation of the content of political speech. Those calling for public financing often point to polls showing public discontent with the high cost of campaigns. The same polls, however, show as much discontent with "too much mudslinging." [55] Indeed, the question, Why should the public pay for ——?, seems a natural response to repugnant, but subsidized, campaign rhetoric.

The existence of subsidies might well decrease citizen participation and the morale of those active in politics. Such was the result in Puerto Rico where, over time, party morale declined and voter interest in party activities was correspondingly reduced. [56] The existence of subsidies, in short, might increase the distance between voters and candidates.

Public financing would also endanger the delicate balance of our party system. If the subsidy were to go largely to party organizations, they would be immensely stronger than they are now. On the other hand, if it were to go directly to candidates, party organizations would be considerably weakened. The subsidy question thus can be rationally decided only after a number of normative as well as empirical

---

[55] The results are from a Gallup poll reprinted in *Hearings*, p. 456.
[56] Committee for Economic Development, *Financing a Better Election System* (New York, 1968), p. 48.

inquiries into the nature of our party system have been satisfactorily resolved. Do we need stronger national parties or stronger state parties? Do we need more candidates independent of existing party organizations, or do we need more organizations such as the Committee to Re-Elect the President? Do we need more party solidarity or will this simply lead to greater executive power?

There are no settled views on any of these questions. Yet the proposals now before Congress threaten to impose a solution to each and perhaps to change our present system radically and rapidly. The danger is not the less because the effect is random or unintentional—or perhaps even mindless.

Similarly, direct subsidization of campaigns must have an enormous but uncertain impact on third parties. If a formula like that contained in the Hart bill is employed, third parties would usually have to gamble whether to take the subsidy. The "seriousness" of a party would have little to do with its decisions since early showings in the polls might augur well—but all third parties suffer late in campaigns from the urge of voters to make their votes "count." Declining the subsidy would be taken to mean that the party was not serious and, in any event, the possibility of subsidy would deter further giving. If the formula is based on showings in previous elections, subsidies would sustain third parties long after their appeal had diminished, simply because they once received a significant portion of the vote.

Direct subsidies would also raise serious problems of freedom of expression. They would be a form of compulsory political activity which limited the freedom of those who would refrain as well as of those who chose to participate. When an individual is forced, in effect, to make a contribution to a political movement to which he is indifferent or which he finds distasteful, it may fairly be said that a basic freedom is being infringed. When this forced payment is combined with limits on contributions to favored candidates, political freedom is drastically limited. Many who today propose subsidies to political parties or candidates condemn subsidies where religious organizations are concerned. The precise constitutional issues differ but they are sufficiently analogous that one may well question whether the underlying principle is not the same. Indeed, what if a religious party were formed?

Public financing of campaigns might run afoul of the Constitution in other ways. Whatever the size of the subsidy, and particularly when combined with a limit on expenditures, the precise amount would be subject to constitutional challenge on the grounds that it discriminated in one fashion or another. The charge would not be less forceful for the fact that it would be entirely up to those in power to say how large the subsidy would be.[57]

Any formula for determining who gets what subsidy is open to constitutional challenge, for subsidies are inherently inconsistent with a "free trade in ideas." One commentator has stated it thus:

> The traditional meaning of this concept is that government must not interfere on behalf of either a majority or a minority; if the majority's superior resources give it greater power to express its views through the mass media, this is a natural and proper result of the superior appeal the majority's "product" has to the public. Government intervention on behalf of minorities would deny first and fourteenth amendment rights to members of the majority group by undermining the preponderance which the free market has given them. Likewise, state action calculated to reduce the relative power of minorities to express their views would infringe their constitutional rights. A plan allocating funds to all parties equally would give minorities publicity out of proportion to the size of their following thus discriminating against the majority, and a plan apportioning funds according to party size would give the majority more funds with which to influence uncommitted voters, tending to increase the majority's preponderance.[58]

This dilemma seems inescapable unless we abandon the tradition that government neither help nor hinder the propagation of the views of a political movement.

---

[57] A subsidy proposed for Massachusetts in 1964 would have allocated $200,000 to the two major parties in proportion to each party's share of the total vote in the last state primary. This formula would have given the Democratic Party the great bulk of the subsidy. An Opinion of the Justices, 347 Mass. 797, 197 N.E. 2d. 691 (1964), however, found the then-pending legislation not to be for a "public purpose" under state law, thus strongly implying that the bill's constitutionality was doubtful.

[58] Note, "Payment of State Funds to Political Party Committees for Use in Meeting Campaign Expenses Lacks a Public Purpose," Harvard Law Review, vol. 78, pp. 1260, 1262-1263. See also Williams v. Rhodes, 393 U.S. 23 (1968). There an Ohio law which made it quite difficult for third parties to get on the ballot was considered. Justice Black, writing for the majority, noted that "there is, of course, no reason why two parties should retain a permanent monopoly on the right to have people vote for or against them. Competition in ideas and governmental policies is at the core of our electoral process and of the First Amendment freedoms." 393 U.S. 32. Similar considerations would seem to apply to a subsidy which gave third parties less than major parties.

3. Summary

Caution in expanding federal regulation of campaign financing seems warranted.

(1) Private campaign money performs both desirable and undesirable functions. No one denies that some campaign contributions are made in the hope of personal gain from the exercise of executive discretion and, as such, are an objectionable, if not illegal, practice. Donors, however, also act from motives which enable contributions to perform functions indispensable to a free and stable political process. The right to give or not to give to a candidate is an aspect of political freedom. Campaign money also acts as an agent of change, permits citizens with little free time to participate in politics, is a vehicle of expression by which individuals seek to persuade others, serves as a barometer of intensity of feeling over potent political issues, and weeds out candidates with little public support. On balance, the undesirable functions of campaign money either call for narrow remedies or are outweighed by the desirable. Contrary to the conventional wisdom, the weight of disinterested scholarship strongly supports this conclusion.

(2) Regulation of the use of campaign money is an undertaking with grave implications for our political freedom. The necessary legislation would have to be passed by those in power and would by its very nature regulate political speech.

(3) Limitations on campaign spending and on individual contributions set a maximum on the political expression in which American citizens can engage and are thus unconstitutional.

(4) The present law requiring disclosure of campaign contributions may chill political activity by requiring that it be registered with the government. By requiring small contributions to be reported, the law seems far broader than is justified by its ostensible purpose and is subject to constitutional challenge.

(5) The arguments made on behalf of public financing of campaigns seem largely unfounded. Public financing might be dangerous, in addition, because no fair formula has been devised for allocating the money and because a subsidy might encourage officials to avoid taking stands on controversial issues. Finally, it would compel taxpayers to engage in political activity against their wishes.

(6) If the question of how campaigns are financed is important, candidates should raise it as an issue, and the people should be allowed to show their opinions by the votes they cast in elections.

Book and cover design: Pat Taylor